For Marni

Reading Consultants

Linda Cornwell
Coordinator of School Quality and Professional Improvement
(Indiana State Teachers Association)

Katharine A. Kane
Education Consultant
(Retired, San Diego County Office of Education and San Diego State University)

Library of Congress Cataloging-in-Publication Data

Meister, Cari.
Catch that cat! / written by Cari Meister ; illustrated by David Brooks.
    p. cm. -- (Rookie reader)
    Summary: Labeled illustrations of a cat in various situations introduce basic words
that are opposites, including "up" and "down," "open" and "shut," and "fast" and "slow."
    ISBN 0-516-21614-7 (lib.bdg.)   0-516-26541-5 (pbk.)
    1. English language--Synonyms and antonyms--Juvenile literature.
[1. English language--Synonyms and antonyms.] I. Brooks, David, 1949–   ill.
II. Title. III. Series.
PE1591.M457 1999
428.1--dc21   98-53056
                                                                                              CIP
                                                                                             AC

1 2 3 4 5 6 7 8 9 10 R 08 07 06 05 04 03 02 01 00

Up.

Down.

High.

Open.

Shut.

Yes.

¡No!

Under.

Fast.

Slow.

Bottom.

Top.

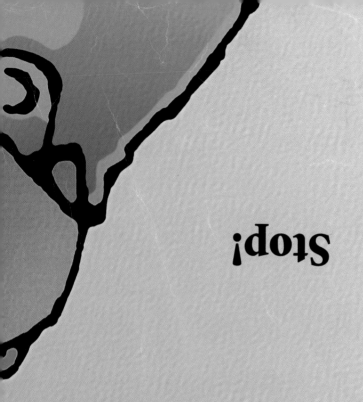

Stop!

Go!

Word List (19 words)

bottom	down	high	open	slow	top
cat	fast	low	over	stop	under
catch	go	no	shut	that	up
yes					

About the Author

Cari Meister loves to write stories about animals—all kinds of animals—cats, dogs, horses, komodo dragons. *Catch That Cat!* is her first Rookie Reader® book. Ms. Meister is also the author of *Tiny's Bath* and *When Tiny Was Tiny* (both Viking). She lives in Excelsior, Minnesota, with her husband John and their dog Samson.

About the Illustrator

David J. Brooks grew up in Pennsylvania, and then moved to Maine, studying art at the University of Maine. He has been a designer and illustrator in Maine for more than twenty years. David now lives in southern California, where it almost never rains.